證果篇

智慧法語

心道

Realization

Interdependence and
the fruition of Buddhahood

多元共生，成就佛果

心道法師 語錄

By Dharma
Master Hsin Tao

目錄

Contents

作者簡介

心道法師一九四八年生，祖籍雲南，幼失依怙，為滇緬邊境孤雛。十三歲隨孤軍撤移來台，十五歲初聞觀音菩薩聖號，有感於觀音菩薩的悲願，以「悟性報觀音」、「吾不成佛誓不休」、「真如度眾生」刺身供佛，立誓

徹悟真理，救度苦難。

二十五歲出家後，頭陀行腳歷十餘年，前後在台北外雙溪、宜蘭礁溪圓明寺、莿仔崙墳塔、龍潭公墓和員山周舉人廢墟，體驗世間最幽隱不堪的「塚間修」，矢志修證，了脫生死，覺悟本來。

生道場」，展開弘法度生的佛行事業，為現代人擘劃成佛地圖。為了推動宗教共存共榮，法師以慈悲的華嚴理念奔走國際，並於二〇〇一年十一月成立世界宗教博物館，致力於各種不同宗教的對話，提昇對所有宗教的寬容、尊重

著重基礎佛法戒、定、慧的學習與薰陶，建立佛法生活規範；「般若期」著重在明瞭與貫徹空性智慧；「法華期」著重生起願力，發菩提心；「華嚴期」則強調多元共存、和諧共生，證入圓滿無礙的境界。

心道法師以禪的

Brief Introduction to the Author

Born in upper Myanmar in 1948 to ethnic Chinese parents of Yunnan Province, Master Hsin Tao was left orphaned and impoverished at an early age. Having

been taken in by the remnants of ROC military units operating along the border of Yunnan, China, he was brought to Taiwan in 1961 when he was 13. At the age of 15, he was

the Buddha, he had himself tattooed with the vows "May I awaken in gratitude for the kindness of Guanyin," "I will never rest until Buddhahood is

enlightenment, Master Hsin Tao traveled on foot for over ten years, practicing austerities in lonely and secluded locations, including Waishuangxi in Taipei, Yuanming

the Fahua Cave on Fulong Mountain in early 1983, Master Hsin Tao undertook a fast which was to last over two years, during which time he attained deep insight into the

Master Hsin Tao felt great compassion for the suffering of all sentient beings. After his solitary retreat he established the Wusheng Monastery on the mountain in order to propagate

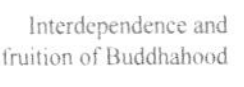

strived hard to gain international support with the compassionate spirit of the Buddhist Avatamsaka Vision (of the interconnectedness of all beings in the universe), and is dedicated to advancing the cause of world peace and a promoting awareness of our global family for love and peace through interreligious dialogues. The

stage training program," a systematic and comprehensive approach applicable to both monastics and lay practitioners alike to help them deepen their practice. First comes the āgama stage, which centers on the foundational teachings of Buddhism and the three-fold practice of morality, concentration, and wisdom. The prajñā

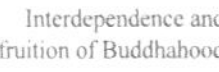

stage emphasizes the theory and practice of emptiness. The dharmapuṇḍarīka stage focuses on the bodhisattva practice of developing the mind of enlightenment through the power

Master Hsin Tao has devoted himself to propagating the Dharma through education, based on the Chan principle of quieting the mind and seeing one's original Buddha-

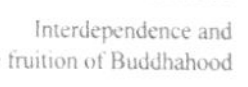

commitment, he leads people to devote themselves to the great cause of benefiting all sentient beings, ceaselessly helping them achieve liberating truth through

心之道第三輯 智慧法語

證果篇-多元共生，成就佛果

The Way of Mind III:
Words of wisdom

Realization :
Interdependence and
the fruition of Buddhahood

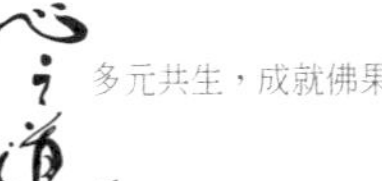

整個世界是相互依存、
多元共生的生命共同體。

Everything
in the entire world
is interdependent;
it's a mutually
interpenetrating community
of life that forms one body.

When the mind is peaceful,
the world is peaceful.

From the perspective of
the Buddha-dharma,
the world is the venue for
awakening.

尊重每一個信仰；
包容每一個族群；
博愛每一個生命。

Respect all faiths, value all cultures, and love all living beings.

Cultivating wisdom and
capacity of mind
leads to
the state free of obstructions,
in which all things are
possible.

愛是我們共同的眞理；
和平是我們永恆的渴望。

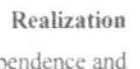

Love is our shared truth;
peace is our eternal aspiration.

The mind is
the Avatamsaka Realm;
the Avatamsaka Realm is
the mind.

人跟人相處，
能懂得溝通對話，
就是智慧的實踐。

Effective communication and getting along well with others is putting wisdom into practice.

成佛由「捨」開始，
能捨棄種種欲望，
便能獲得內心的寂靜
與安定。

The path to Buddhahood begins with renunciation; renouncing all desires, you gain inner peace and tranquility.

If you can regard
all sentient beings as
the Buddha, then you are
on the path to Buddhahood.

Light can't penetrate the mind which only perceives darkness.

With a tranquil mind,
you can perceive
the beauty and
brightness of life.

見到自己本來的面目，
蘊化天地和諧與
世界和平的能量。

Recognize your original face, manifest the power of harmony and peace throughout the world.

Everyone who practices Buddhism has the ability to generate bodhicitta and attain Buddhahood.

擁有禪的寧靜與
慈悲的願行，
必能共振出世界和平。

The peace and goodwill generated in meditation resonate throughout the world.

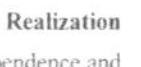

Interreligious cooperation is all about selfless giving.

Use meditation
to harmonize the mind;
use compassion
to care for the world.

眾善奉行，
讓生命、生活就像在
極樂世界一般。

Through the power of wholesome action, life becomes like a paradise.

點燃正念正覺，
就能使善業永續。

Generating mindful awareness leads to endless blessings.

成佛的願力和
成佛的路就是慈悲，
華嚴世界就是
從慈悲開始做起。

Compassion is the way to
Buddhahood;
it's also the way to
the Avatamsaka Realm.

世界因差異而存在，
因同而和諧。

The world arises
out of differentiation;
harmony arises
out of sameness.

成佛大道
必須生生世世耕耘，
才能堅固，
反覆無常就不行！

The attainment of
Buddhahood
requires steadfast cultivation
life after life;
occasional practice
is not enough.

以了脫生死爲目的；
以成就佛法者爲榜樣。

Make liberation from saṃsāra your goal in life; take eminent practitioners of the Buddha-dharma as your role models.

Promoting peace and
global ethics
is the way to manifest
the Avatamsaka Realm.

皈依三寶，
坐上佛法的渡船離開苦海，
到達極樂世界。

Take refuge in the Triple Gem; take the boat of Dharma across the sea of misery and reach the land of perfect bliss.

人人做好心靈環保，
建立善業，
就能幫助地球平安。

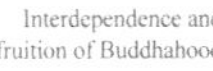

Spiritual environmental protection means practicing goodness and caring for the Earth so that there may be peace.

生起善念，
去除執著與分別，
以清淨無染的心念，
實踐成佛的菩提大願，
這是最圓滿的
供養與迴向。

Cultivate wholesome thoughts;
eliminate attachment and
discrimination;
use the mind of purity
to realize Buddhahood;
this is the greatest contribution
anyone can make.

沒有對立的世界就是
禪的世界；禪的世界
就是華嚴的呈現。

Meditation is the way
to create a world
without conflict;
this is how to manifest
the Avatamsaka Realm.

Recollecting misery generates misery; recollecting happiness generates happiness; recollecting the Buddha generates Buddhahood.

以謙卑和尊重
連結宗教大愛，
面對苦難，
轉換貪婪，
化解暴力與衝突。

Use modesty and respect to manifest love, face suffering, transform miserliness, and overcome violence and conflict.

只有世界融洽
才能拯救地球，
人心才會快樂。

If you want to save the world, start by cultivating harmony and understanding. This is the way to happiness.

By planting wholesome seeds in your own mind, you encourage others to do the same; this is an awakened approach to life.

念佛就是一點一滴
供養十方諸佛，
累積足夠功德，
最後成就華嚴世界。

Recollection of the Buddha means cultivating merit by continually paying homage to the Buddhas of the ten directions; the final result is the manifestation of the Avatamsaka Realm.

Selfless giving,
harmony, and faith are
the concrete expressions of
the Global Family of
Love and Peace.

「識」是分別心；
「智」如日月遍照一切，
能夠轉識成智，
即是華嚴世界。

The mind of wisdom illuminates the entire world, just like the sun and moon; transforming the mind of discrimination into the mind of wisdom is to create the Avatamsaka Realm.

「華」是智慧，
「嚴」是排列，
「華嚴」就是佛國
就是智慧的排列。

Concerning Avatamsaka
(Chinese: *Huayan*):
hua means "wisdom,"
yan means "array";
the Avatamsaka Realm is a
Buddha land,
an array of wisdom.

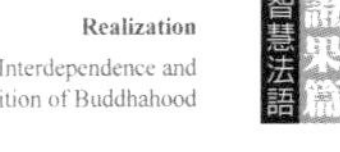

Use meditative concentration to enter into wisdom, awakening, and the equality of the Avatamsaka Realm.

能夠心開意解，
對生命奉獻，
就不會起貪、瞋、癡。

When you open your mind,
cultivate understanding, and
practice generosity,
you no longer generate
greed, hatred, and delusion.

With the mind of
enlightenment,
allthe world becomes like a
flower in a mirror or
the moon reflected in water
- as if an illusion.

每個緣都是我們的業力，
面對它，灌溉它，
爲它播下正覺成佛的種子。

Like a seed,
every action has
the potential to bring
future results;
with this in mind,
plant the seeds of
awakening.

交流、對話是尋求
生命共同價值的方法。

Interaction and dialogue are a way of identifying shared values.

以大悲心為體，
成就正等正覺的果位。

Use the mind of great compassion to attain perfect enlightenment.

Illuminate your mind,
recognize your inherent nature,
practice the teaching of the
Buddha — this is
the way to awakening.

Use faith to find stability;
practice goodness;
purify your mind;
make the Pure Land
a reality.

Transform inner tranquility into outer peace.

Those matured in the Buddha-dharma are beyond harming others.

When the mind is tranquil, then the world is peaceful.

止惡行善、
平等慈悲、
自利利他，
是學佛人要奉行的
倫理原則。

Refraining from evil,
doing good;
equanimity and compassion;
benefitting self and others
— this is the foundation of
Buddhist ethics.

眞正的尊重來自於
無我，
最大的包容來自
對空性的明白，
眞實的博愛是
對無盡緣起的體悟。

True respect comes from selflessness;
great embracing comes from insight into emptiness;
genuine love arises out of the experience of dependent origination.

心之道第三輯智慧法語
證果篇-多元共生，成就佛果

心道法師語錄
總 策 劃：釋了意
主　　編：洪淑妍
責任編輯：林玉芬
英文翻譯：甘修慧
英文審校：Dr. Maria Reis Habito
美術設計：蒲思元
發 行 人：歐陽慕親
出版發行：財團法人靈鷲山般若文教基金會附設出版社
劃撥帳户：財團法人靈鷲山般若文教基金會附設出版社
劃撥帳號：18887793
地址：23444新北市永和區保生路2號21樓
電話：(02)2232-1008
傳眞：(02)2232-1010
網址：www.093books.com.tw
讀者信箱：books@ljm.org.tw
法律顧問：永然聯合法律事務所
印刷：大亞彩色印刷製版股份有限公司
初版一刷：2014年7月
定價：新台幣250元(1套4冊)
ISBN：978-986-6324-76-5
總 經 銷：飛鴻國際行銷股份有限公司

靈鷲山書網

The Way of MindⅢ：Words of wisdom

Realization：Interdependence and the fruition of Buddhahood

Words of Dharma Master Hsin Tao
General Planer: Ven.Liao Yi Shih
Editor in Chief: Hong, Shu-yan
Editor in Charge: Lin, Yu-fen
English translator: Gan, Xiu-hui
English Proofreading: Dr. Maria Reis Habito
Art Editor: Pu, Szu-Yuan
Publisher: Ouyang, Mu-qin
Published by and The postal service is allocated: the Subsidiary Publishing House of the Ling Jiou Mountain Prajna Cultural Education Foundation
Account number: 18887793
Address: 21F., No.2, Baosheng Rd., Yonghe Dist., New Taipei City 23444, Taiwan (R.O.C.)
Tel: (02)2232-1008
Fax: (02)2232-1010
Website: www.093books.com.tw
E-mail: books@ljm.org.tw
Legal Consultant: Y. R. Lee & Partners Attorneys at Law
Printing: Apex Printing Corporation
The First Printing of the First Edition: July 2014
List Price: NT$ 250 dollars(Four-Manual Set)
ISBN: 978-986-6324-76-5
Distributor : Flying Horn International Marketing Co., Ltd.

國家圖書館出版品預行編目(CIP)資料

心之道智慧法語. 第三輯 / 洪淑妍主編. --初版.
-- 新北市 : 靈鷲山般若出版, 2014.07
冊 ; 公分
ISBN 978-986-6324-76-5(全套 : 精裝)

1.佛教說法 2.佛教教化法

225.4 103011796